# FUNNY MAN DAN

# JOKES OF SOME SILLINESS

### Jokes for EVERY situation

# C+TY
# V-NE

First published in Australia by City & Vine

Text Copyright © 2025 by Daniel Lee-Archer

Daniel Lee-Archer asserts the moral right to be identified as the author of this work in accordance with the Copyright, Designs and Patents Act 1988

A catalogue record for this book is available from the National Library of Australia

Paperback ISBN
978-1-922411-44-0

Ebook ISBN
978-1-922411-49-5

Illustration by Ric Sugitha at eOne Design
Cover and book design by eOne Design

www.cityandvinebooks.com

# CONTENTS

Being funny is not just about having the best joke, but when you tell a joke that perfectly fits in your situation, that is funny. **Like Really Funny.**

Amaze your family, friends, and firefighters (I just needed another people group that started with the letter F) with this book of Jokes for Every Situation.

# 1

## Dentist

Going to the dentist can be a bit scary,
so why don't you lighten the mood
with these great jokes - just don't make
the dentist laugh whilst they
are holding the drill!

**1** What is the best time to see the dentist?
**Tooth-Hurty**

**2** What do you call a dentist that doesn't like tea?
**Denis**

**3** What type of tea do all dentists hate?
**Cavi-tea**

**4** What do you call someone who takes children's teeth from under their pillows and wakes them up with a 'Boo'?
**The Tooth Scary**

**5** Why did the dentist join the army?
**To become a drill sergeant**

**6** Why did the king go to the dentist?
**To get a new crown**

**7** What does a dentist do on a roller coaster?
**He braces himself**

**8** Why did the dentist go to the North Pole?
**To see a molar bear**

**9** What does the 'Dentist Of The Year' get?
**A little plaque**

**10** Why was the band member's teeth so clean?
**He had a big tuba toothpaste**

**11** How do dentists advertise their services?
**By word of mouth**

**12** What did the patient say to the dentist after his 50th appointment?
**I know the drill**

**13** What is a dentist's favourite dance?

**The floss**

**14** Why did the boy have some string in his sandwich?
**The dentist told him to floss between meals**

**15** Which nationality was the very first dentist?
**Polish**

**16** Why did the dentist have teeth x-rays at his party?
**In case someone needed a tooth-pic**

**17** What is a dentist's favourite dinosaur?
**A Flossiraptor**

**18** Why is a dentist nothing like a restaurant?
**They don't offer free refills**

**19** Why should you never lie to a dentist?
**Because they always know what the tooth is**

**20** Why did the Pharaoh visit the dentist?
**Because Egypt his tooth**

# 2

## Soccer / Football

Football or Soccer - no matter what you call it, it's the most played game in the world. Whether you're playing, spectating or refereeing, use these jokes and your friends will definitely get a 'kick out of it'.

**1** What hot drink do goalies all hate?
**Penal-tea**

**2** Why did the goalie fix the broken bench in the locker room?
**She was the only one allowed to use her hands**

**3** Why do soccer players have so much fun?
**They always have a ball**

**4** What does a football player and a bull have in common?
**They both get angry when they see red**

**5** Why do soccer players do so well in school?
**They know how to use their heads**

**6** How do you stop squirrels playing football in the garden?
**Hide the ball, it drives them nuts**

**7** What football club do sheep like?
**Baaaaaaaaaa-rcelona**

**8** Which goalie can jump higher than the crossbars?
**All of them, crossbars can't jump**

**9** Why can't you play soccer with pigs?

**They hog the ball**

**10** Why did the football team spin around and around in circles?

**They wanted to win the Whirl Cup**

**11** What runs around a soccer field but never moves?

**A fence**

**12** Why did the hopeless goalie get in trouble at school?
**He never saved his work**

**13** Why is Cinderella so bad at soccer?
**Because she had a pumpkin for a coach**

**14** Why is a soccer stadium the coolest place to be?
**Because it's full of fans**

**15** Why did the soccer player bring string to the game?
**So she could tie the score**

**16** How do we know that soccer referees are happy?
**Because they whistle while they work**

**17** Why did the coach order long sandwiches during the game?
**He needed more subs**

**18** Do grasshoppers like football?
**No, they prefer cricket**

**19** What happened to the soccer ball that made a mess in a restaurant?
**It got kicked out**

**20** Why did the lady marry a soccer player?
**Because he was a keeper**

# 3

## School

School is a fantastic place to learn, grow and even have some fun along the way. With these amazing jokes, you can laugh while you learn.

**1** Why did the boy take a ladder to school?
**He wanted to get into high school**

**2** Which subject is the saddest?
**Math, it's full of problems**

**3** What do you call a science project that doesn't work?

**A Volcan-NO**

**4** Why didn't the balloon want to go to school?
**In case there was a pop quiz**

**5** Why could the King always draw a straight line?
**Because he was a ruler**

**6** Why did the teacher have to wear sunglasses?
**Because her pupils had become so bright**

**7** What happened to the music student who rearranged the notes?
**He got in treble**

**8** What did the teacher do when he went to Hawaii?
**He tested the water**

**9** Why did the math student find it hard to learn decimal places?
**They couldn't get the point**

**10** What is the sweetest type of school?
**Sundae school**

**11** Where do maths teachers go on vacation?
**Times Square**

**12** What is the best way to get straight A's?
**Use a ruler**

**13** Why was the school student jealous of Adam and Eve?
**Because they didn't have to study history**

**14** What was the name of the girl who always knew when school was about to start?
**Wendy Bellrings**

**15** What type of school do surfers attend?
**Boarding school**

**16** Why did the teacher tie everyone's shoe laces together?
**So they could go on a class trip**

**17** Why did the principal bring his Ikea furniture to school?
**For the school assembly**

**18** What is a runner's favourite school subject?
**Jog-graphy**

**19** Why should you never talk to a pencil sharpener?
**Because they always go around and around until finally they get to the point**

**20** Why did the child bring a napkin and cutlery to math class?
**They were going to learn about Pi**

# 4

## Library

A Library is the only place in the world where you can sail the seven seas, solve unsolvable mysteries and find a strange little man wearing red and white striped clothes in a sea of chaos. Be careful, these jokes may make your friends laugh so much you hear a loud shhhhhhhh.

**1** Why are libraries the tallest buildings in the world?
**They have the most stories**

**2** Why did no one know about the opening of a new library?
**Because it was kept hush-hush**

**3** Where should you never go when you need to hear the truth?
**The liebrary**

**4** Why couldn't the girl find a book about magic in the library?
**Because they all disappeared**

**5** What did the librarian say to the little round vegetables that were making noise?
**Quiet peas**

**6** What do librarians like to cook on the BBQ?
**Shhhh-kebabs**

**7** Why did the man want to borrow a book, while getting a hotel room, while seeing the doctor?
**So he could Check Out. In and Up at the same time**

**8** What book did the cat borrow from the library?
**The Prince and the Paw-Purr**

**9** Why did the librarian throw away the book about milk?
**It had past its shelf life**

**10** What did the library give the lady who was 9 & ½ months pregnant?

**A fine for being overdue**

**11** Did you hear about the librarian who had a book fall on top of his head?

**He only had his shelf to blame**

**12** Why did the librarian retire?
**She was ready for a new chapter**

**13** What was everyone saying about the new book 'Mount Everest'?
**It was a real cliff-hanger**

**14** What's everyone saying about the new book 'Anti-Gravity'?
**It's impossible to put down**

**15** Why did the man fall over in the library?
**He was walking through the non-friction section**

**16** Why couldn't the librarian go to the party?
**They were fully booked**

**17** What do you call a sunburnt librarian?
**Well red**

**18** Why did all of the books on the shelf have no covers?
**It was the mystery section**

**19** Why did the library have a mirror installed?
**For those people who wanted to self-checkout**

**20** Why do librarians use book carts?
**That's just how they roll**

# 5

## Dinner Time

There's something wonderful about
sharing a meal with your family
and friends. Make dinner time even
more fun with this smorgasbord of
delicious jokes.

**1** What is the only thing you can't eat at dinner?
**Breakfast and lunch**

**2** Why is dinner at the baby goat farm so crazy?
**There are way too many kids**

**3** Why did the child hate German sausages?
**She thought they were the wurst**

**4** Why was the cheese allowed to cook his own dinner?
**Because he was very mature**

**5** Do you want to know the recipe for gold soup?
**Take any normal soup and add 14 karats**

**6** What did the kid say to his dad who went to drink milk that had been left out for 3 days?
**Spoiler alert**

**7** Why should you be very careful when someone slides you the milk?
**Because it can fly pasteurise and onto the floor**

**8**
Why do eggs never tell jokes at the dinner table?

**In case they crack up**

**9** What is the world's easiest diet?
**The see-food and eat it diet**

**10** What did the locksmith make for dessert every night?
**Cook-keys**

**11** Why didn't the boy want to eat the rabbit stew?
**There was a hare in it**

**12** Why is it easy to cook dinner for a dalmatian?
**Because it always hits the spot**

**13** Why could the fungi family only fit 2 of them at the table?
**They each needed as mush-room as possible**

**14** Why can you order snails for dinner at most places in France except for McDonald's?
**They only serve fast food**

**15** Why should you never let a comedian cook you dinner?
**Their food tastes funny**

**16** What did the skeleton order for dinner?
**Spare ribs**

**17** What always smells the best at dinner time?
**Your nose**

**18** What is a frog's favourite type of dinner?
**Stir flies**

**19** What does a giant sea monster eat for dinner?
**Fish and ships**

**20** Did you hear the joke about the pizza?
**Don't worry, it's too cheesy**

# 6

## Going To The Park

A trip to the park is a wonderful way to spend your weekends or time after school. Take these jokes with you on your next trip and getting a laugh will be a walk in the park.

**1** How do you make a swing go really, really high?

**Take away the S**

**2** What do the monkeys, lions and tigers like to do at the park?

**Play on the jungle gym**

**3** What do all shoes like to play at the park?
**Sock-er**

**4** Why is Nicolas always the first chosen to play every game at the playground?
**Because everybody loves to pick-nick at the park**

**5** Why didn't the robber play basketball with his friends?
**He didn't want to go to court**

**6** Why was the man looking at 100 deer through his binoculars?
**He was herd watching**

**7** Why did the subway go to the park?
**Because so many people go there to train**

**8** Why did the family drive straight past the playground?
**Because they couldn't find a park**

**9** Why did the man cook a stir fry outside in nature?
**He wanted to have a wok in the park**

**10** Why was Superman the only one allowed on the play equipment?
**Because of the sign that said 'supervision needed'**

**11** Why did the chicken cross the playground?
**To get to the other slide**

**12** Where was the sleepy dad's favourite place in the park?
**The restrooms**

**13** Why didn't the child enjoy flying their kite?
**Too many ups and downs**

**14** Why did the boy put some bread on his kite?
**He was fishing for birds**

**15** Why did the lady wear a fancy dress to play sports with her friends?
**She was told there would be a ball**

**16** What does a presentation and a playground have in common?
**They both have a least one slide**

**17** Why didn't the council buy the big slide for $1,000?
**It was a bit too steep**

**18** Why did they make a movie about a hot dog at the park?
**So it could be an Oscar wiener**

**19** Why did the boy bring cookie dough to the park?
**Because his mum said she was going there to sunbake**

**20** What do a family of lions do before having a picnic?
**They take some time to prey**

# 7

## A Trip To The Zoo

If you love animals, there is no
better place to visit than the zoo.
While you are there you can't go
wrong with any of these jokes,
because they're all keepers.

**1** How did the apes escape the zoo?
**They had a mon-key**

**2** Why do all zoos open late?
**They always have a lion**

**3** Which animal should you never play games with?
**The cheater**

**4** Why do zoos keep water animals?
**So they can get a seal of approval**

**5** Which animal makes the best comedian?
**A gir-laugh**

**6** Why did the koala become the manager of the zoo?

**He had the right koala-fications**

**7** Why was the sandwich on display at the zoo?
**It was bread in captivity**

**8** What kind of bird can you find at both a zoo and a construction site?
**A crane**

**9** Why can't a leopard hide?
**Because he's always spotted**

**10** What do you call an angry monkey?
**Furious George**

**11** Where do the animals go to learn martial arts?
**A jujit-zoo**

**12** I once saw a movie about a zoo with only giraffes.
**It was called Giraffic Park**

**13** What do you call an elephant with an extra long nose?
**A smellephant**

**14** What happened when the zoo shut down its bear exhibit?
**It made the whole place un-bearable**

**15** Why do giraffes have such long necks?
**Because their feet smell**

**16** What do you get when you mix an elephant and a kangaroo?
**Big holes all over Australia**

**17** Why did the grizzly throw away his socks?
**Because he had bear feet**

**18** Which zoo animals grew up in Bangkok?
**The Thai-gers**

**19** What did the buffalo say to the boy when he dropped him off at school?
**Bison**

**20** What do you call a zebra in the ocean?
**A seabra**

# 8

## Travel - Train

Whether it's a trip to school or a vacation to the countryside, train travel is so much fun. But long travel can be a challenge to keep things fun. So use these jokes to derail any boredom.

1. What did the mother train say to her child at dinner?
**Make sure you chew chew**

2. Why do comedians only ride on monorails?
**Because they love one liners**

3. When is it not safe to read between the lines?
**At a train station**

4. How do you find out how heavy a whale is?
**By taking it to the whale weigh station**

5.

How does a cow travel across the country?

**In a loco-mootive**

**6** How does toothpaste in London like to travel?
**On the tube**

**7** What happened to the man who took the 5pm train home?
**He had to give it back**

**8** Why are train engineers not scared of being electrocuted?
**Because they aren't conductors**

**9** Why are railways so good at transport?
**They train thousands of times a day**

**10** What does an inspector ask for on the frog train?
**Crickets please**

Moo! Moo! Moo!

**11** How do you find a missing train?
**Follow the tracks**

**12** Why was the train engine humming?
**It didn't know the words to the song**

**13** Why did the boy ask for a toy railway for Christmas?
**He wanted a play station**

**14** Why did the engineer put a rocket on the last carriage of the train?
**To give it a caboost**

**15** What type of trains travel fast and furiously?
**Vin Diesel trains**

**16** Which transport system is the smallest?
**Subways - they only come in 6 inch or 1 foot**

**17** What do you call a train that can't stop sneezing?
**Achoo-choo train**

**18** What do you call an angry dog on a train?
**A passen-grrrrrr**

**19** How did the man go as fast as the train?
**He was sitting in it**

**20** Why was the train easily distracted?
**It kept getting side tracked**

# 9

## A Trip To The Trampoline Park

Who doesn't love a trampoline?
Well, a whole park of trampolines is
multiple times the fun. Here are some
great trampoline jokes to help you
spring into action.

**1** Why did the man put a sheep on a trampoline in winter?

**He needed a woolly jumper**

BAA!

**2** What happened when dad switched his bed for a trampoline?

**Mum hit the roof**

**3** Is jumping on a trampoline fun?
**Yes, but it has its ups and downs**

**4** Why did the parents want their daughter to study to be a trampoline instructor?
**Because it was something for her to fall back on**

**5** What happened when the trampoline park was having tough times?
**It bounced back**

**6** When is the most dangerous time of year to jump on a trampoline?
**Spring break**

**7** Why do the flowers at the trampoline park bloom all year round?
**It's always springtime**

**8** Why did the security guard go to the trampoline park?
**He wanted to be a bouncer**

**9** Why did the cow jump on a trampoline?
**She wanted to make a milkshake**

**10** What's the best thing to drink at the trampoline park?
**Spring water**

**11** What did the dad say when the trampoline park closed?
**Time to bounce**

**12** What happened when the store had a deal for half-price trampolines?
**Everybody jumped on it**

**13** Why was the boy scared of trampolines?
**They always made him jump**

**14** Why did the dad make his shoes out of trampolines?
**He wanted to go to work with a spring in his step**

**15** What happened when the trampoline park had to close early?
**Everybody flipped out**

**16** Have you seen the movie about a bouncy dog?
**It's called 'Lady and the Trampoline'**

**17** Why don't you ever have to wait at a trampoline park?
**Because it's so easy to jump the queue**

**18** Why did the man push his car to the trampoline park?
**To give it a jump start**

**19** Why couldn't the twins go to the trampoline park?
**Because there was no double bouncing allowed**

**20** What is a candy bar's favourite trick on the trampoline?
**A snack flip**

# 10

## Birthdays

Who doesn't love a birthday?
Unlike all of us, these jokes will
never grow old.

**1** What did the man buy his wife for her birthday when she asked for lots of diamonds?

**A pack of playing cards**

**2** Why were the parents surprised when it was their twin's birthday?

**They had to do a double-cake**

**3** What should you never do at a slice of bread's birthday party?

**Make a toast**

**4** Why was the dirt celebrating?
**It was his earth-day**

**5** Who did the horse invite to his birthday party?
**His neigh-bours**

**6** What did the dynamite do when he got his birthday cake?
**He blew up his candles**

**7** Why did the knight ride around and around the kingdom on his birthday?
**He wanted to play pass the castle**

**8** Where is the best place to find a present for your feline friend?
**In a cat-a-log**

**9** What does the hulk get for his birthday every year?
**A SMASH cake**

**10** Why couldn't the teddy bear eat any more cake?
**He was stuffed**

**11** What did the pirate say a year after he turned 79?
**Aye matey**

**12** When will a cake cause you to feel sick?
**When you take away the C**

**13** Why did the girl put her cake in the freezer?
**She wanted extra frosting**

**14** Why are crabs great to invite to your party?
**They really know how to shell-ebrate**

**15** What do clones sing on their birthday?
**Happy birthday two me's**

**16** When does the postman celebrate his birthday?
**Everyday, he is always playing pass the parcel**

**17** Who is the only guest that doesn't like birthday parties?
**The piñata**

**18** What is the coolest type of birthday cake?
**Ice cream cake**

**19** What present is guaranteed to light up anyone's face?
**A lamp**

**20** Why do we put candles on the top of birthday cakes?
**Because they don't fit on the bottom**

# II

## Travel - Plane

A trip on a plane is a great adventure. Whether you are going on a vacation or visiting relatives that live far away, these jokes are all guaranteed to land.

**1** What happens when you wear a watch on a plane?
**Time flies**

**2** What must you do on a candy plane before take-off?
**Fasten your treat belt**

**3** Why did the confused egg farmer bring his bird to the airport?
**He was told there was a chicken desk**

**4** How does a rabbit travel?
**On a hare-plane**

**5** Why was everyone on the plane grumpy?
**They all had a bad altitude**

**6** Who invented the first-ever aeroplane that couldn't fly?
**The wrong brothers**

**7** What do you call a policeman wearing a pilot uniform?
**A plane clothes cop**

**8** What noise does a low flying plane piloted by a cat make?
**Meeeeeeeeeeeeeeeeeooooowwwww**

**9** Why did the pilot have trouble making friends?
**People didn't think she was down to earth**

**10** Why should you always do your homework on an aeroplane?

**So you can get higher grades**

**11** Why did the pilot in training fly through a rainbow on his test?

**So he could pass with flying colours**

**12** Why didn't the boy laugh at the aeroplane joke?

**It flew over his head**

**13** What do you call a doughnut on a flight without any toppings?

**A plain plane doughnut**

**14** Why couldn't Snoopy and Charlie Brown get anything to eat on the plane?

**Their flight didn't serve peanuts**

**15** Why doesn't Sonic like to travel on planes?

**He suffers from motion quickness**

**16** Where do bees like to travel on vacation?

**To Stingapore**

**17** Have you heard about the book that all pilots have to read?

**It's called 'Flying a Plane' by Landon Safely**

**18** What do you call a plane made out of rubber?

**A boing 747**

**19** What does an aeroplane engine and an air conditioner have in common?

**If they stop working, people start to sweat**

**20** How did the man drop his phone off a cliff only to find it later without a scratch?

**He had it on airplane mode**

# THE HALF-TIME SHOW

## The Importance of Timing

The difference between a good joke and one that is not well received is often in the timing.

Here are some handy hints to help you with your 'ha ha's' ...

# ① Pick the right place

Some places are great to get a laugh, like on the playground at lunch, or at your mate's place after school. Others are not so great such as:

In the middle
**of the night**

In the middle **of class**

In the middle **of the desert**

Basically, avoid anywhere in the middle of something.

# ❷ Choose the right audience

A great audience are those who love to laugh and are expecting to hear something funny. A not so great audience could look like:

A superhero fighting bad guys

A pilot trying to land a plane

A patient at the dentist

# 3 Select the right situation

The right joke about the right topic in the right situation is just amazing. It will make people laugh and enjoy what they are currently doing even more. But not all jokes fit all situations, such as:

Eating at the table

Why did the boy throw up his meal?

The good news is that with this book you will always have a great joke for every situation*

*As long as you only ever find yourself in 22 situations or until future volumes of this joke book come out.

# 12

## Baseball

Baseball - a wonderful American sport enjoyed by many all around the world. Next time you are watching or playing a game, these jokes can help you strike up a conversation full of laughs.

**1** Why did the police come to the ball game?
**Because someone had stolen the bases**

**2** Why did the outfielder bring a swatter to the game?
**In case there was a fly ball**

**3** Why do twins make such good batters?
**They're always getting doubles**

**4** Why did the baseball player jog around his living room?

**To practice his home runs**

**5** Why did the batter carry a locked box with him to the base?
**So he could always be safe**

**6** What does an umpire say when you leave his house?
**Yoouuu'rrrrre OUT**

**7** Which baseball player also holds the team's water?
**The pitcher**

**8** Why did Cinderella never play for the Major League?
**She would always run away from the ball**

**9** Why were the failing baseball team always sweating?
**They had lost all their fans**

**10** Why did the teams have to play baseball at night?
**Because their bats slept during the day**

**11** Which two fictional characters are the best at baseball?
**Batman & Homer Simpson**

**12** Why did the matchstick stop playing baseball?
**After one strike, he was out**

**13** What do a baseball team and a pancake recipe have in common?
**They both need great batters**

**14** What did the baseball glove say to the ball?
**I'll catch you later**

**15** Why are baseball stadiums so expensive?
**Look at the size of their diamond**

**16** Why did the batter go to the playground?
**To spend some time on his swings**

**17** Why did the baseball player go to the supermarket for 5 minutes?
**It was a shortstop**

**18** Why do retired baseball players come back to the stadiums from time to time?
**Just to touch base**

**19** Why did the batter put a peg on his nose?
**In case he hit a foul ball**

**20** Why does a pitcher raise one leg when pitching?
**If he raised any more he would fall over**

# 13

## Going To The Doctor

Going to the doctor is not always a fun experience. If you or someone you know is not feeling well and has to go to the doctor, cheer them up with these jokes. They do say laughter is the best medicine!

**1** Why are doctors great at jigsaw puzzles?
**They have lots of patients**

**2** What do you call a doctor who fixes websites?
**A URL-ologist**

**3** What did the doctor say to the patient who broke their arm in two places?
**Stop going to those places**

**4** What did the doctor do for the patient that stepped on some Lego?
**He gave him something to block out the pain**

**5** Why did the comedian study to become an obstetrician?
**So he could deliver both jokes and babies**

**6** Why did the tonsils get dressed up?
**The doctor promised to take them out**

**7** Why did the banana go to the doctor?
**He wasn't peeling well**

**8** Why did the calendar go to the doctor?
**It had a terrible year-ache**

**9** Why did the doctor keep away from the shop?
**It was an apple store**

**10** Why did the woman bring her computer to the doctor?
**It had a virus**

**11** Why did the balloon go to the doctor?
**It was feeling light-headed**

**12** Why did the cookie go to the doctor?
**He was feeling crummy**

**13** What did the doctor tell the boy with a carrot in his ear?
**You're not eating properly**

**14** What did the doctor tell the patient who kept seeing Mickey, Minnie and Pluto?
**You are having Disney spells**

**15** Why did the doctor give the patient 23 different pills to take each day?
**Because she wasn't drinking enough water**

**16** Why did the rope go to the doctor?
**It had a knot in its stomach**

**17** Where do sick boats go to get healthy?
**To the dock**

**18** What parts of playing doctor with Dad are no fun?
**At the start when he makes you wait 45 minutes and at the end when he sends you a bill**

**19** Why did the priest take his church's old keyboard to the hospital?
**Because he was an organ donor**

**20** What did the doctor tell the person who couldn't sleep?
**Lie on the edge of the bed and you will soon drop off**

# 14

## A Trip To The Beach

What a wonderful way to spend the day
with your friends and family at the beach.
So pack your towel, swimwear, hat,
sunblock and these jokes which will make
your experience go swimmingly.

**1** Why is the ocean so much friendlier than a pool?
**The pool never waves**

**2** What do you call a person who can fix any type of sandcastle?
**A sandy man**

**3** Why was the kid excited to go to the beach?
**Her parents said she could have as much sun-screen time as she wanted**

**4** Why was the surfer embarrassed?
**Because his shorts caught a rip**

**5** What do you call a puppy at the beach?
**A hot dog**

**6** Why was the safety-conscious swimmer covered in sand?
**He was swimming between the flags**

**7** What do you call a polar bear at the beach?
**Lost**

**8** What do you get if you cross the Red Sea on a blue bicycle?
**Wet**

**9** What did the beach say when it was asked if swimming was allowed?
**Shore**

**10** Which celebrity lives at the beach?
**A starfish**

**11** Why do seagulls fly over the sea?
**Because if they flew over the bay, they would be bagels**

**12** What kind of tree fits in your hand?
**A palm tree**

**13** Why didn't the sun go to college?
**He already had a million degrees**

**14** What's the best day of the week to go to the beach?
**Sun-day**

**15** Why did the dad beg his boy to come to the beach?
**Because the beach is no fun without the son**

**16** What happened when the beach party got out of hand?
**It was sandemonium**

**17** Why did the boy pick up all of the seaweed at the beach?
**He was trying to be kelp-ful**

**18** What did the lifeguard say when everyone was swimming safely?
**It's shore perfection**

**19** Why did the chef bring an oven to the beach?
**So they could do sun baking**

**20** What did the beach owner call out to his friends?
**Come on in, the water's mine**

# 15

## The Aquarium

The oceans contain over 1 million different types of sea creatures and animals. Lucky for us, we don't need to go diving as we can visit many of them at our local aquarium. Next time you're there share these jokes and everyone will be otterly entertained.

**1** What do you need to make an octopus laugh?

**Exactly ten-tickles**

**2** Why was the aquarium awarded the best-run business award?

**Because it was very e-fish-ant**

**3** Which country's aquarium has the most sharks?

**Finland**

**4** What type of shark has been viewed billions of times?
**Baby Shark**

**5** What did the fish in the tank say to the other fish?
**Do you have any idea how to drive this thing?**

**6** What do octopuses say when you try to prank them?
**Are you squidding me?**

**7** Why did the lobster apply for a job at the pizza place?
**So he could work at the crust-station**

**8** Why did the aquarium close down the day before their new dolphin show?
**For training porpoises**

**9** What happened when two turtles crashed into each other while swimming?
**It was a turtle disaster**

**10** What do they say to you when you are leaving the aquarium?
**Sea you next time**

**11** What happened when the aquarium opened the new electric eels exhibit?
**Everyone was shocked**

**12** Why are fish so smart?
**They live in schools**

**13** How does a seahorse get around the aquarium?
**They scallop**

**14** Why did the penguin take a pickaxe to parties?
**It was a great icebreaker**

**15** Why do clownfish never get eaten?
**They taste funny**

**16** How can you tell which fish are teenagers?
**They are always on their shell-phones**

**17** Why was the fish put in time out?
**Because he was gill-ty**

**18** Why don't you have to weigh fish at the aquarium?
**Because they all have their own scales**

**19** Why can you always trust a marine mammal with a secret?
**Because their lips are sealed**

**20** What do you call a sea cow that makes fun of you?
**A Manatease**

# 16

## Travel - Car

Travelling by car is a normal part of a
lot of people's lives. Next time you find
yourself in an automobile, I have
a bunch of fantastic jokes that you
will never get tyred of.

**1** Why did the car fall over?
**It went on a road trip**

**2** Which car was really good at painting?
**Vincent VAN Gogh**

**3** What car is the sweetest ride?
**A Ferrari rocher**

**4** How do cars choose the best restaurants?
**They look at the acceleratings**

**5** Why did the frog catch the bus?
**His car got toad**

**6** What do you call a cow driving a car?
**A fast mooooover**

**7** What has four wheels and flies?
**A garbage truck**

**8** What do heart doctors and car salesmen have in common?
**They are both car-deal-ologists**

**9** What is small, green, wise and powerful and can travel up to 200 miles per hour?
**A toy-yoda**

**10** Where do dogs park their cars?
**In the barking lot**

**11** What's a car's favourite meal?
**Brake-fast**

**12** Why is it so funny to drive through the mountains?
**They are hill-areas**

**13** What happened when two French cheese trucks crashed into each other?

**Everyone was ok but there was de-brie everywhere**

**14** Why did the man think he had a magic car?

**Because every time he drove home it turned into a driveway**

**15** Why did the car cough all night?

**So the next day he could have more hoarse-power**

**16** Why did the child need to wear gloves when playing with his toy cars?

**Because they were Hot Wheels**

**17** What was wrong with the wooden car?

**It wooden go**

**18** What do cars do when they get so old that all of their wheels are completely worn out?

**They retire**

**19** What do motorhomes say on long road trips?

**RV there yet?**

**20** Why did Henry invent the car after he upset his wife?

**So he could give it to her and ask for Ford-give-ness**

# 17

## A Trip To The Farm

A farm is a wonderful place to visit.
Filled with interesting animals
and fantastic people who live a lot
differently to city folk. Next time you're
on a farm try out these jokes on anyone
who has ears (including the corn).

**1** What place on the farm do you get the best wifi reception?

**The barn, it has a stable signal**

**2** How does a gardener drink his water?
**By using a straw-berry**

**3** Where does a farmer keep his stationery?
**In his pig pen**

**4** Why did the cow say goodbye to his friends?
**He was moooving**

**5** Why did the farmer work really hard?
**So he could reach the crop of his field**

**6** Why was the farmer so good at drawing circles?
**Because he rides a pro-tractor**

**7** Where do kids start learning how to be a farmer?
**In kinder-garden**

**8** Why couldn't the cow trust the goat?
**Because he was always kidding**

**9** How do chickens make cakes?
**From scratch**

**10** Why did the horse get sick after his dinner?
**He got hay-fever**

**11** Why should you never pamper a cow?
**You don't want spoilt milk**

**12** Why was the farmer embarrassed when his cattle kept telling jokes?

**They were a laughing stock**

**13** Why did the chickens put on a show for the whole farm?

**Because it was a great form of hentertainment**

**14** What farm animal will always show up just at the right time?

**A watchdog**

**15** What time do the ducks get up in the morning?

**At the quack of dawn**

**16** Where does Old MacDonald get his medicine?

**At the farm-acy**

**17** What is a sheep's favourite sport?

**Baaaadminton**

**18** What happens when you say 'Hey' to a horse?

**They reply 'Yes, please'**

**19** What do you call a sleeping bull?

**A bull-dozer**

**20** How many sheep did the farmer have?

**No one knows, when anyone tries to count they fall asleep**

# 18

## Snow Day

Here are some jokes you can use next time you're playing in the snow that will make you look cool.

**1** What did the snowman say to the other snowman?
**Do you smell carrots?**

**2** Why did the girl set up a movie theatre in the snow?
**She wanted to watch Frozen**

**3** What do you eat when you are angry in the snow?
**A brrrr-grrrr**

**4** What happened when the snowman got angry?
**He had a meltdown**

**5** How does a snowman get to work?
**By icicle**

**6** What do snowmen call their offspring?
**Chill-dren**

**7** Why should you not make fun of the cold weather?
**It's snow joke**

**8** What do you get if you celebrate your birthday at the North Pole?
**A cake with lots of frosting**

**9** Why did the actor move to Antarctica?
**Because there is no business like snow business**

**10** What do you call a snowman with a six pack?

**An abdominal snowman**

**11** What's a snowman's favourite game?
**Ice Spy**

**12** What did the snowman do at the weekend?
**Nothing, he just chilled**

**13** How do polar bears write thank you notes?
**They use a pen-guin**

**14** How did the penguin make sure his house stayed together?
**Igglued it**

**15** What does Batman put in his drink?
**Just-ice**

**16** What do you call an old snowman?
**Water**

**17** Why shouldn't you give Elsa a balloon?
**She will let it go**

**18** What is the best way to deal with the news of an incoming snowstorm?
**With a million grains of salt**

**19** Why should you never take your catchers mitt out in the snow?
**In case you catch a cold**

**20** Why did the kid put his dad's vitamins in the snow?
**So he could give him a chill pill**

# 19

## Gymnastics

Gymnastics is a fun sport to compete in and watch. Next time you're with a gymnast tell them these jokes and they will flip out.

**1** How did the gymnasts feel after they won a medal?
**They were beaming**

**2** How does a gymnast read a PDF?

**Using Adobe Acrobat**

**3** What is a gymnasts favourite drink?
**Anything served in a tumbler**

**4** Why was the gym equipment crooked?
**It was a trampo-lean**

**5** Why was the number two gymnast sad?
**They weren't allowed on the uneven bars**

**6** What is a gymnast's favourite dessert?
**A banana split**

**7** What did the gymnast say when they were disqualified?
**That's not fair, it wasn't my vault**

**8** What does a failed gymnast and a supermarket have in common?
**They both have bad cartwheels**

**9** How did the gymnast add flavour to their meal?
**They put on somersalt**

**10** Why is gymnastics the most competitive sport?
**They would all bend over backwards to win**

**11** Why did the gymnast's parents have to put them to bed three times?
**They wanted a triple tuck**

**12** How did the gymnast feel when she won a medal for the best backflip?
**She was head over heels**

**13** Which Disney princess is a secret gymnast?
**Ariel**

**14** What happens when you put down a mat that goes all the way outside the door?
**Everyone flips out**

**15** How long does it take a gymnast to get ready for practice?
**A split second**

**16** When is the best time of year to buy a trampoline?
**Spring time**

**17** Why did the bank call the gymnast?
**Because they had outstanding balance**

**18** What is a gymnast's favourite fruit?
**A pommel-granite**

**19** Why did the gymnast give his fellow competitors hats made out of mops?
**So he could wipe the floor with his competition**

**20** Why did the gymnast get upgraded to business class?
**Because they were a frequent flyer**

# 20

## Family
## Board Game Night

There's no better place to build great
memories than a family board game
night. Get out all of your favourite games,
gather your family, use these jokes and
SNAP, you have family fun all around.

**1** What is the best game to play after a fight?
**Sorry**

**2** What is a cat's favourite game?
**Mouse Trap**

**3** What game do parents hate when their kids play it?
**Trouble**

**4** Why should you never throw scrabble pieces at each other?

**Somebody could lose an I**

**5** What is a fun game but also helpful in getting out stuck food between your teeth?
**Toothpicktionary**

**6** What is the best game to play on your way to work?
**Trivial commute**

**7** What is the number 1 game in all Spanish speaking countries?
**Uno**

**8** Which game wouldn't let the family play it?
**DomiNOs**

**9** Which game can't you play in a big city?
**Monopoly, because there is no such thing as free parking**

**10** What game do The Avengers play at dinner time?
**Hungry Hungry Heroes**

**11** What game do dare-devils play all the time?
**Risk**

**12** Which board game can you play at the playground?
**Ticket to slide**

**13** What game do butchers like to play at work?
**The game of knife**

**14** Why did the board game enthusiast order some Ikea furniture?

**He wanted to play connect drawer**

**15** What's the best game to play while going down a slide?

**Yaht-weeeeeeeee**

**16** What game do sunbathers like to play at the beach?

**CaTAN**

**17** What game do DIY enthusiasts like to play?

**Handy land**

**18** What game can you play with a packet of Doritos?

**Battle Chip**

**19** Which game are architects forbidden to play?

**Jenga**

**20** What is extreme winds favourite game?

**Twister**

# 21

## Ten Pin Bowling

It's always fun to go Ten Pin Bowling.
Next time you strap on your bowling
shoes and grab your ball, tell these
jokes and no one will be still standing
(even if the pins are).

**1** What do the pins do when they're not happy?
**They go on strike**

**2** Why did the baseball player have to leave the bowling alley?
**He just got his third strike**

**3** What do you call it when you knock down the pins you missed with a pocket full of coins?
**Spare change**

**4** Why was the house cleaner terrible at bowling?
**They were always cleaning out the gutters**

**5** What do you call it when you throw a camera but it doesn't knock down any pins?
**Shutter ball**

**6** Why should you never play bowling against extreme weather?

**7** Why do clowns love bowling alleys?
**It's the only place that has sillier shoes than they do**

**8** What do bowlers and thanksgiving have in common?
**They both love getting turkeys**

**9** Why was the cat always bowling?
**Because he was an alley cat**

**10** Who is the best at curving the ball in the whole of Neverland?
**Captain Hook**

**11** Where is the best place to get a custom bowling uniform?
**New Jersey**

**Because lightning always strikes**

**12** Why did the man work at the bowling alley for just a few weeks?

**He was only ten-pin**

**13** Why can't you go bowling with a champion player?

**They have no spare ball**

**14** Why did the bowler get to the alley before his team?

**To get the ball rolling**

**15** What did the bowling ball say as it was racing towards the pins?

**Don't stop me now. I am on a roll**

**16** What did the wife tell her husband who wouldn't stop talking about how he knocked all the pins over in two bowls?

**Spare us the details**

**17** What do bowling alleys and libraries have in common?

**At both of them you can hear a pin drop**

**18** Why did the mother show her kids she loves them by knocking down all the pins in two goes?

**Because sparing is caring**

**19** Why did everyone know who the bowler was?

**Because he is frame-ous**

**20** What is a bowler's favourite snack?

**Skittles**

# 22

## Bedtime

At the end of every day comes bedtime. If you're like me you will try everything to stay up for a few minutes more. Try out these jokes on your parents and they might not be able to rest-ist.

**1** What happened when the boy woke up after dreaming of eating a giant marshmallow?

**He couldn't find his pillow**

**2** Why did the farmer fall asleep in the field?

**He was counting sheep**

**3** Why did the famous composer love going to bed?
**He had award-winning sheet music**

**4** What did the mother cow say to her child?
**It's pasture bedtime**

**5** Why shouldn't you share a room with a scuba diver?
**They love to snore-kel**

**6** Why should you be quiet at a library?
**Because the books are all sleeping under their covers**

**7** Why was the letter E fired from his job?
**Because he was always in bed**

**8** Why did the bicycle stay in bed all day?
**Because he was two tyred to get up**

**9** Why is sleeping so easy?
**You can do it with your eyes closed**

**10** What did the kitten wear to bed?
**Paw-jamas**

**11** What happened to the egg who stayed up all night?
**The next day he was egg-hausted**

**12** How did the dad burn 2000 calories whilst sleeping?
**He took a nap with a pizza in the oven**

**13** What did the worm do at 5 am to save his life?
**He went back to bed**

**14** Why did the man sleep under his car?
**He needed to wake up oily**

**15** Why did the woman fall asleep holding her phone?
**She downloaded a nap**

**16** How do you stop someone from sleepwalking?
**Send them to bed with a bicycle**

**17** Which animal can you always see sleeping on a safari?
**A ZZZebra**

**18** Why did the boy sprinkle sugar on his bed?
**So he could have sweet dreams**

**19** Why does Mum call Dad 'Simba' on Saturday mornings?
**Because he is the lie-in king**

**20** Why was the actor extremely happy to get the role of the sleeping man?
**It was his dream job**

# OTHER RESOURCES

## Songs of Some Silliness

Join Funny Man Dan as he sings 20 of his favourite and funniest songs in one colossal collection. Giggle at his song about Gifts, Cackle at Crazy Noise and be delighted with 'Dandy Candy Eating Handy Hands'.

## Funny Man Dan Live: Hello

I'm sure you've seen stand-up comedy, but when you are in front of thousands of kids, standing may not be enough. Recorded live in front of thousands of kids in Sydney, Australia, Funny Man Dan brings his zany antics and bright green shirt to your living room. After discovering that none of his jokes were needed because he could make kids laugh with a single word, Funny Man Dan embarked on a journey of developing what he calls 'Bounce Around' comedy. This live performance includes a preschool show, sure to delight toddlers and the headline show that will have your school-aged kids in stitches.

# About Funny Man Dan

Dan Lee-Archer started busking with circus performers as a teenager on the streets of Tasmania (Tasmania is the small island down the bottom of the really big island Australia). After moving to Sydney with the hopes of becoming a famous actor (which may still happen according to his Mum); he somehow stumbled upon the opportunity to perform in front of children at conferences and big events. This was a match made in heaven as the kids found everything he did (and what he looks like) hilarious, and Funny Man Dan was born.

After two hilarious decades and millions of laughs, he is now a writer, producer, actor, singer-songwriter, YouTuber and Kids and Families performer for audiences all over the world.

He also tells everybody he loves sushi,
but that seems a bit fishy.

www.ingramcontent.com/pod-product-compliance
Lightning Source LLC
Chambersburg PA
CBHW060032050426
42448CB00012B/2968